# HELP IS ON THE WAY

FOUR LAKES POETRY SERIES

GENERAL EDITOR

Ronald Wallace

# Help Is on the Way

John Brehm

The University of Wisconsin Press

The University of Wisconsin Press
1930 Monroe Street, 3rd Floor
Madison, Wisconsin 53711-2059
uwpress.wisc.edu

3 Henrietta Street
London WC2E 8LU, England
eurospanbookstore.com



Printed in the United States of America
Library of Congress Cataloging-in-Publication Data

Brehm, John, 1955–
Help is on the way / John Brehm.
p. cm.—(Four lakes poetry series)
Poems.
ISBN 978-0-299-28624-8 (cloth : alk. paper)
ISBN 978-0-299-28623-1 (e-book)
I. Title. II. Series: Four Lakes poetry series.
PS3602.R444H45 2012
811'.6—dc23
2011041957

for

George Masahiro Brehm

1981–2009

## *Help Is On the Way*

*Time heals all wounds*
*except those*
*it*

*in-*
*flicts—and*
*in time even those.*

# Contents

# Acknowledgments

My thanks to the editors of the following journals for first publishing some of the poems collected here.

*The Best American Poetry blog:* "On the Subway Platform"
*Barrow Street:* "A New Addiction Please"
*Boulevard:* "Fourth of July," "Conflagration"
*The Cortland Review:* "Wind Over Water"
*The Gettysburg Review:* "Valid Photo Identification Required," "Of Love and Life Insurance"
*Gulf Coast:* "Full Circle," "One Way or Another"
*The Manhattan Review:* "First and Last"
*The Missouri Review:* "Lineage"
*New Ohio Review:* "Help Is On the Way"
*Poetry:* "So Long," "Pompeii," "Passage," "Getting Where We're Going," "Over and Under"
*Rattle:* "Dear Internal Revenue Service"
*The Sun:* "Newborn, Brovetto Farm"
*This Land:* "Critical Mass," "Prophecies: Right Here, Right Now"

Deep gratitude also to these friends and poets who helped make this a better book: Dana Elkun, John Kadlecek, Marilyn Krysl, Greg Kuzma, Radha Markum, Fred Muratori, Douglas Schniztpahn, and Ted Stein. Special thanks to Mike Henry and Andrea Dupree, and to everyone at Lighthouse Writers Workshop.

# I

# Over and Under

# Pompeii

Standing on the subway, exhausted, dispirited,
glancing over the exhausted, dispirited faces
of my fellow passengers, I read posters
for a new movie about Pompeii.
"How can you breathe when the air is on fire?"
"How can you escape a boiling mudslide?"
"How can you outrun an eruption
faster than this train?" they ask.
Obviously the ad writer has never been
on *this* train, because this is a Q train,
and anybody who can't outrun a Q train
must be on death's doorstep anyway
and will soon be overtaken by time itself,
if not a boiling mudslide, though sometimes
that's what time feels like, thick
and burning, pushing you on and pulling
you back. And now we rise creaking
over the Manhattan Bridge, where
one can see through scratchy windows
the city skyline and the buildings that are
not there, where thousands tried
to breathe air on fire and failed,
tried to flee an avalanche of concrete
and falling bodies and failed.
If only they'd been asked to outrun something
as slow as this slow train that takes us home—
how easily they might have done it.
But that is not what they were asked to do.

# Prophecies: Right Here, Right Now

Today it's a guy hawking prophecies on the 4 train.
Strides into the car at the Brooklyn Bridge stop,
white hair, huge, thick, scholarly glasses,
a bristling, steel-wool, Whitmanesque beard,
and starts in about the Book of Revelation.
Has a stack of Xeroxed prophecies in his hand
as he walks up the aisle. "Only God knows
the future," he says. "Man knows nothing
of what awaits him. That's why he acts
like such a fool. No man can predict the future.
If you know of someone who ever has,
please tell me, I'd like to hear about it."
"Nostradamus," I almost blurt out
from my half-slumber, but I could tell,
or thought I could, that he'd have an answer
for that. Nor did I wish to incur his wrath.
I had a brief vision of him hectoring
above me while I burst into flames
and the other passengers shifted in their seats
and looked away, or kept on reading
their *Posts* and *Daily News*, where the prophecies
he's raving about are now being fulfilled,
with the help of U.S. tax dollars.
"The meek shall inherit the earth," he says.
"And the meek are the poor. Blessed are the poor,
and woe to the rich, that's what the Bible says."
And now I'm recalibrating how crazy I think he is.
He's certainly playing to the right crowd.
The people on this train look like their
only inheritance thus far has been
more poverty, rage of exclusion and fear
of their own rage. "Look at the African American
in South Africa," he says, as if reading my mind.
"What could a man 3,000 years ago know
about South Africa, let alone the African American?
*Nothing!* And yet prophecies of the African American
in South Africa are right here in the Bible."
And here, too, I think of correcting him.
Africans are in South Africa, African Americans

in America, though white people have done their best
to divide the suffering equally between them.
But maybe I'm misunderstanding
the prophecy in question. "There are prophecies
on every page of the Bible. *Every page!*"
he shouts at our departing backs,
and shakes the stapled pamphlets in the air.
I wonder what his life is like when he's not here
spreading God's word to commuters
lost in our underground limbo, hurtling
into our shaky, unforeseeable futures. And I wonder
now as he slides backward into my memory
what other dazzling configurations
of craziness and wisdom are taking shape,
readying themselves to appear before us.
He's right. I can't imagine them.

# Critical Mass

Lifted their bikes up-
side down above
their thousand
heads and
cheered
locked the grid
blocked the inter-
section shut
the whole East
Village down
cars jammed
against that
stopped moment
that break in
time's flow
nothing moving
nowhere
to go unless
inward until
the helicopter's
searchlight shook
the air and cops
billyclubbed
a couple kids
to set example
hauled off
a truckload of
others forced
apart the forces
that swirled
together there—
but what I still see
are the wheels
held upward
spoked with light
freed from
the pavement
spinning into sky.

# Valid Photo Identification Required

I don't understand myself, nor do I know myself, nor
can I explain or prove who I am to anyone else.
All I know is that I'm a man who let his out-
of-state Driver's License expire and who
does not have his original Social Security Card,
(issued at birth?) or a copy of said document,
to obtain which one must have an unexpired
Driver's License, which requires, of course, a valid
Social Security Card. I needed something to get me
on a plane at LaGuardia. I did have a Birth Certificate,
and when I slid it tentatively under the bullet-proof
Plexiglas window at the Brooklyn Social Security Office
and said "What about this?" to the unexpectedly
sympathetic and ontologically sophisticated young
Asian American man scanning my application
for a replacement card, he looked at me and said:
"This doesn't help. This just proves you were born.
We need proof of your *continued* existence."
I threw up my hands and looked down at my body,
as if to say, Well, I'm standing here, aren't I?
I admit I have not done much with this life.
I have failed at love, let down my friends,
ignored my best instincts and given my worst ones
free play, but for better or worse I *have* continued
to exist. Because if I *hadn't* continued to exist
I wouldn't be contemplating all the joys and deep
satisfactions of nonexistence, as I am right now.
I don't imagine the dead are required to show papers
at every river crossing, or that only those with valid
photo ID are allowed into the caldron, or the
harpsichord concert, as the case may be. Often I wake
at 3 a.m., I wanted to tell him, with the night terrors,
scrambled fears of death, which would be one
of the privileges conferred exclusively upon the living,
and often I wish I could forget myself completely,
forget the fragile, worried, rabbit-hearted self
that seems to run my life, forget the whole
nightmarish mess—I wouldn't have *that*
feeling if I hadn't continued to exist, would I?

It's true, I wanted to confess, I have no children
to mirror me into the future, and mostly I only
half-inhabit the poems I've written, a ghostly
uneasy absence floating just below the lines.
In fact, from the Buddhist perspective
I don't exist, but neither do you, nor any of this.
A luminous emptiness is all there is.
Instead I tell him I just want to visit my parents,
for Christmas, in Nebraska, for christsakes.
Which was no help.

# First and Last

Back pain all night long a little preview
of old age sickness and death and
devil-spawn of unanswerable
questions does pain persist past this
life and insomnia is that something
I should worry about over there
same kind of night I have here
stretched to an abject infinity
and what about self-inflicted utterly
meaningless loneliness surely I won't
drag that with me into the beyond
people say death makes life more
poignant well sure it does bone-
shakingly so and a lot more
miserable too as if poignancy
at once consolation and consequence
were somehow worth it my father's
hands shake he can barely walk
who built this house himself fifty
years ago dug the foundations poured
the concrete framed it laid the brick
roofed and shingled and
finished it and yes it's poignant
but I'd rather he live forever
people will say anything in this
grainy dreamworld we will all be
parted from and you can't blame
them any more than they blame
themselves talking's what makes
us human that and our dark
foreknowledge which is probably
what made us open our mouths
shape them into sounds
in the first place.

# Of Love and Life Insurance: An Argument

"I need to accept you as you are," she said,
"so you need to become the kind
of person I can accept." I was
becoming bewildered, but I don't
think that's what she meant.
"Life Insurance," she said. "You
don't have any Life Insurance."
"But we've only known each other
three months. Aren't we jumping ahead?"
"Look," she said, "I don't want
to have to take my child and move
back to Chicago and live with my mother.
I don't want to have to take my child
to a public clinic. And I don't want to
have to ride you and nag you and ask you
a hundred times about all this stuff."
And then my heart fell from the sky
like a shot bird. "Is *that* how you
imagine a life with me?"
I guess being an unsuccessful poet
isn't as attractive as it used to be.
But where's the risky spirit,
the headlong leap into the vast
unknown of love, where anything
and everything might happen? Where's
the wish to be surrounded by poems,
the great sustaining luxuries and dangers
of poems, or to make one's life itself
a poem, unpredictable, meaning
many things, a door into the other world
through which even a child might walk?
Words have such power, I wanted to tell her.
You never know what may come of them.
Or who will be the beneficiary.

# Talk of the Town

I wonder how many words are generated
each day here in New York City.
If eight million people speak
roughly the national average
of 7,000 words a day,
or slightly more since
New Yorkers like to talk,
that comes to over 56 billion
per day in the five boroughs,
and this is not counting all the words
that thank God go *un*spoken,
which if you added them in
would take the total well
into the trillions, nor all
the words that are written,
which I cannot bear even
to contemplate, and if words
had visible shapes they'd clog the air
like the birds John Muir said were
so numerous they blackened
the skies over nineteenth-century
America before we got the hang
of killing them. But what
happens to them, these
little puffs of mindstuff,
where do they go, how do
they change us and what
would be the effect of
just one day of utter silence
here in New York City?
Would the city melt away like
the illusion it probably is,
or rise up, released at last
from the weight of our
speech and thought,
or simply stand clear
in all its wounded dignity
and squalor, without our words
to cover it up, our words
that make the whole world appear
and disappear at the
same time.

# Getting Where We're Going

Surfeit of distance and the wracked mind waiting,
nipping at itself, snarling inwardly at strangers.
If I had a car in this town I'd
rig it up with a rear bumper horn,
something to blast back at the jackasses
who honk the second the light turns green.
If you could gather up all the hornhonks
of just one day in New York City,
tie them together in a big brassy knot
high above the city and honk
them all at once it would shiver
the skyscrapers to nothingness, as if
they were made of sand, and usher
in the Second Coming. Christ would descend
from the sky wincing with his fingers
in his ears and judge us all
insane. Who'd want people like us
up there yelling at each other, trashing
the cloudy, angelic streets with our
candywrappers and newspapers and coffecups?
Besides, we'd still be waiting for
the next thing to happen in Heaven,
the next violin concerto or cotton-candy
festival or breathtaking vista to open
beneath our feet, and thinking this place
isn't quite what it's cracked up to be,
and why in hell does everybody
want to get here? We'd still be
waiting for someone else to come
and make us happy, staring
through whatever's in front of us,
cursing the light that never seems to change.

## Change in Service

"Attention passengers, there is no uptown
local service on the 1 train at this time.
Repeat, there is no uptown
local service on the 1 train at this time.
For uptown local service, transfer
at 14th Street across the platform
to the downtown number 2 train.
Take the downtown number 2 train
to Chambers Street. At Chambers Street,
transfer to shuttle bus service
for South Street Ferry. At South
Street Ferry, take a Circle Line
Sightseeing Cruise Ship up
the East River to the 59th Street Bridge.
At the 59th Street Bridge, fling
yourself overboard and swim
to Roosevelt Island.
From Roosevelt Island, take
the Tramway back to Manhattan.
Exit the Tramway
and take a cab to the FDR
Expressway. Proceed north
on the FDR Expressway
to the George Washington Bridge.
Cross the George Washington Bridge
and take the Palisades Parkway
north to Piermont. At Piermont,
rent a kayak and paddle down
the Hudson River to 96th and Riverside.
From 96th and Riverside
walk east to Central Park West,
turn right on Central Park West
and proceed south to Columbus Circle.
At Columbus Circle take a rickshaw
to 42nd Street Times Square.
At 42nd Street Times Square, ride the escalator
down past the Fellini-esque organist
with the swiveling, trumpet-
playing monkey dolls
and board the uptown local 1 train,
which is now running on the downtown

number 2 express track across the platform.
Return to 14th Street and begin again.
Have a nice day and thank you
for riding the MTA."

# Dear Internal Revenue Service

Thank you for your letter informing me of the errors
in my 2005 filing. I'm enclosing a check for
$5,657 to cover the tax which I evidently
still owe and the interest on that tax.
I would hereby like to ask, however,
that you forgive the penalty of $1,136
since the employer failed to send me a 1099
for the income I made as a consultant that year.
Of course I realize it's my responsibility to report
all my income, but in the absence of a 1099
I simply forgot. I have a number of clients
and I'm (obviously) not the best bookkeeper.
Nor am I particularly "good with money."
I am a poet as well as a freelance writer,
and being a poet isn't quite as lucrative
as you might imagine. You may notice,
for example, that for all of last year I received
$57 in royalties. (A friend of mine helpfully
observed that I could have made more money
"as a parking meter," to which I replied that
I could have made *a lot* more money as a parking meter,
and gotten a lot more respect as well.)
Unlike most hard-working poets in America,
I don't teach, mainly because I don't know anything.
I'm probably not all that far from the clichéd notion
of the romantic poet you yourself may hold.
I get stoned sometimes and stare at trees and clouds
for hours on end, try to see the wind, etc.
I weep for no reason, remember real or imagined
slights for ages, and lick my wounds with words.
I live in a studio apartment, a garret, if you will.
I have a huge desk—it's like the deck of a ship,
and I its landlocked captain, gazing out to sea.
It sits underneath my sleeping loft, which
my girlfriend likes to call "the lofty loft,"
for reasons I won't go into here as they may seem
inappropriate, or too personal, or perhaps
irrelevant to my purpose, which is to ask your
forgiveness of the penalty and to offer reasons why
by explaining the hardships of the poet's life.
I'll just say that sometimes it gets pretty lofty up there

and sometimes we imagine we're on a magic carpet
drifting smoothly above the city below, in its state
of semi-controlled, slow-motion collapse,
and on out over the ocean, which she loves and fears,
just like I do, or over the summer-campy Catskills,
where we can't afford to buy a country house,
with their worn-down mountains and charmingly
self-effacing trees, so unlike the impossibly massive
and overly serious cedars and hemlocks and
Douglas fir trees of the Pacific Northwest,
where I used to live until poverty forced me East.
Those trees are brooders—dignified, mist-shrouded
monsters—beautiful, of course, and awe-inspiring
(I wonder if you have felt this), but too damply
archaic and imposing and uncomprehendable
for my taste. I like a tree you can take in with
a single steady gaze. I wonder if you are as bad
at poetry as I am at accounting. Perhaps we are
the inverted mirror images of each other.
I don't imagine you get asked that question
very often or receive many letters like this one.
Maybe you're reading this out loud even now
to your office (I almost said "cell") mates. Of my book
a reviewer once said that "you simply can't resist
reading many of these poems out loud to someone else,"
and I wonder if you feel this—the irresistible
need to read this poem aloud. I'm sure
the letters you receive are mostly angry ones,
the kind that say things like, "Here, take my
Goddamn money and buy Dick Cheney a few more
gallons of puppy blood for his nightly ablutions,"
or "Dear IRS, please use the enclosed check to
purchase some hand-held rocket-launchers to blast the fuck
out of some poor Iraqi's house, which you prefer
to call 'a suspected insurgent stronghold.'"
Or, "Please give this money to the CEO of Exxon
so he can buy silk socks while I regurgitate
my supper and try not to starve."
I thought of taking that approach, I felt
that desire to get in a shot or two, to give voice
to righteous indignation, treat you like
a nonperson, someone mindlessly
and heartlessly saying "no" all day long.

But I'm done with all that, I want to reach you,
to speak to you as a fellow human being immersed
in the same joys and suffering as I am—didn't you
once write poems yourself, poems of anguish
and loss and loneliness?—and to remind you
of the karmic delights of forgiveness that
await you if you release me
from this debt.

# Fourth of July

Freedom is a rocket,
isn't it, bursting
orgasmically over
parkloads of hot
dog devouring
human beings
or into the cities
of our enemies
without whom we
would surely
kill ourselves
though they are
ourselves and
America I see now
is the soldier
who said I saw
something
burning on my
chest and tried
to brush it off with
my right hand
but my arm
wasn't there—
America is no
other than this
moment, the
burning ribcage,
the hand gone
that might have
put it out, the skies
afire with our history.

# Newborn, Brovetto Farm

for Chris

Just under the dairy
farm's hayloft
a four-day-old calf—
big, soft, earth-
colored eyes,
looks exhausted,
slightly affronted,
hard-skulled
already but other-
worldly, world-
weary, as if it had
been here many
times before
and was none too
pleased to be
back as a cow
in this cow-hating,
cow-devouring,
cowardly country.
"Next time, try
coming back
as a poet," I
wanted to say.
"Then we'll talk."

Or maybe I should
try coming back as
a cow so I could
appreciate, retro-
spectively, my
present good fortune.
I think I was an
orangutan once,
perhaps a scorpion,
possibly also
a slave or a murderer.
But never a cow,
in America,

where the dis-
assembly lines at
slaughterhouses
move so fast
the animals
don't have time
to die and so are
hacked apart, still
struggling to escape.
This one, at least,
will have a pasture,
and be milked
instead of killed,
fed well, probably
even talked to.
Still, I felt her
trapped intelligence,
saw the shoulder-
shrug look of rotten
luck in her eyes,
and the wish to be
elsewhere, the wish to
return and begin
again, I'd forgotten
I knew so well.

# A New Addiction Please

Trollopian nonsense but the branches
outside my window lit like chalices,
emptied of everything and
therefore full—the president
said last night we are addicted to oil
and the strange sound of truth
almost dropped me, like hearing
a crack dealer say cocaine
might be bad for us, why don't
we get addicted to wind or sunlight,
then we'd be properly trafficking
in the invisible, energized by
the unseen, uncapturable,
unuseupable source of all life
instead of sucking up the death-juice
of dinosaur bones or ripping
the heads off mountains
in Appalachia, we're already
addicted to wind and sun, who
could live without them?
and I think someone should
name all the types and textures
and strengths and meanings and
origins and typical destinations
of all the winds in the world,
I would like to have that job if
it's ever created, so on my passport
it would say Cataloger of Winds,
or Windographer, or just Mr. Breezy,
how much better that would be
than Writer or Poet! and I would
be allowed into any country without
question and would spend my days
on mountaintops with my eyes
shut and my hands gently out-
stretched and when people
wanted to use some winds to drive
their cars or power their lawn-
mowers or light up their living rooms
where the family sits awkwardly
saying nothing but seething

underneath with rage and rotting
sexual desires, they'd have to
consult me and I'd tell them which
winds would work best to take
them where they need to go,
or to shine a light on what
they wish or do not
wish to see.

# One Way or Another

Being this calm makes me
nervous, because I know
calamity gathers
strength in such weather,
that pain sharpens
itself against the hard
edge of happiness,
just as joy digs itself
out of disaster.
A year ago I told
a friend that my
shrink said if I really
wanted to deal with
all my "obsessive-
compulsive stuff"
I'd have to take an SSRI,
one of those floaty-
sounding drugs
like Prozac or Zoloft
that turn the mind
into a trampoline
of optimism and
the penis into a sullen,
slouching spectator.
"Are you thinking
about it?" she asked.
"Yes," I said. "I can't
*stop* thinking about it."

But I decided against it.
I fell in love instead,
saw a chance to polish
my relationship-ruining
skills to a perfect
self-consuming shine,
and took it.
Tried to turn hunger
itself into a feast
that would last forever
and worried my way
from bliss to loneliness

in just under a year.
But now I'm fine.
Totally calm.
Yesterday I heard
the first three notes
of a cardinal's song and
thought it was a car alarm.

# Wind over Water

You can never get enough of what you don't need,
that's true, but you can sure spend some time
trying. All my life piling one emptiness
on top of another to build a house even
the slightest wind will collapse. And that wind
comes nearly every day. One can feel it
forming deep in mountain stillnesses.
*There are no fish in the lake,* the Dhammapada
tells us. *The long-legged cranes stand in the water.*
I think I know why they'd do that.
It's cool and clear and the reflection
of the flight that brought them here lingers
in the air like a trace memory above them.
They find their being in the fish not being there.

# Revelation

My memory is like a steel-toothed trap
and my memories like bewildered animals
lured from the thick of the forest
by strong scents and caught here now
howling and bitten with regret
for all their innocence, their stupidity,
their hunger and their great mistakes.
In the morning I will gather them,
club them if they are not yet dead,
skin them and stitch them into a coat
to keep myself warm and admired and concealed.

# Passage

In all the woods that day I was
the only living thing
fretful, exhausted, or unsure.
Giant fir and spruce and cedar trees
that had stood their ground
three hundred years
stretched in sunlight calmly
unimpressed by whatever
it was that held me
hunched and tense above the stream,
biting my nails, calculating all
my impossibilities.
Nor did the water pause
to reflect or enter into
my considerations.
It found its way
over and around a crowd
of rocks in easy flourishes,
in laughing evasions and
shifts in direction.
Nothing could slow it down for long.
It even made a little song
out of all the things
that got in its way,
a music against the hard edges
of whatever might interrupt its going.

# So Long

To break this day
free from all
the others

to stand at the
morning end
of it and

push off from
the shore
sail beyond

the reach of all
my failures
calling after me

"You can't just
leave us here"
shaking their fists

crowding into
the water
clamoring "We

made you who
you are" to
feel their voices

growing small
underneath
the surf

the wide un-
knowable ocean
all before me.

# Conflagration

Soon the green
flames of
the sycamore
will set
the sky on fire
now that
the buds
have been lit—
sometime
in the darkness
overlapping
and under-
lying the day
it happened
and now
sunlight
catches them
and they
leap up into
sight—the
whole world
must have
begun like this
love begins
like this
burning leaving
nothing
as it was before.

# Full Circle

Serpentine tautologies sing out from spaces
where silence is just another kind of singing
and things come to mean just what we
want them to here in this city where any
moment millions of people are moving
underground and millions more lofted
into the unlooked-at sky imagine still
other worlds far from these streets that fill
with the flickering energies of thoughts
sweeping upward or hovering just
above eye-level of the pedestrians'
roaring speechless procession every inter-
section a supercollider an atom smasher
of interior monologues rich and strange
here where to breathe the air is to inhale
the thin harsh music of the consciousness
of the city itself and to know the dog-
eared book of its moods and imaginings
dog-eared book of days left open on a table
by a window where wind turns the pages
because that's what wind likes to do.

# On the Subway Platform

for Kate

Where are you going I said
and she said I'm going

to look for a book
and I said what kind

of book? A book on
PERFECTIONISM

she said and I said
make sure you get

the right one—
which brought forth

such perfect laughter
from her perfect heart.

# Over and Under

So sexy to slide under-
neath a river,
to sit inside this
snakelike sub-
marine-like
subway car and
freely imagine
the world above—
the Brooklyn
Bridge invisibly
trembling with the
weight of its
own beauty,
the East River
still guided by
the grooves
Walt Whitman's
eyes wore in it,
the bulldog tug-
boats pushing the
passively impressive
broad-bottomed
barges around,
and the double-
decker orange
and black Staten
Island Ferries,
with their aura
of overworked
pack-mule
mournfulness,
and beyond them
the Atlantic Ocean
which I lately learned
was brought here
by ice-comets three
billion years ago,
which explains
a few things, like
why everybody
feels so alienated,

and of course
the thoughts being
thought by every
person in New
York City at
this moment—
vast schools of
undulating fish
curving and rising
in the cloud-swirling
wind-waved sky,
surrounded by
the vaster emptiness
of nonthought
which holds them
and which they try
not to think
about and you
lying in bed in
your sixth-floor
walk-up sublet
on St. Mark's Place—
such a breath-
taking ascension!
imagining me
rising now to meet you.

# II

# Still Falling

# Lineage

I

When we fell down from the trees, that's
when we learned to feel and
feel afraid on the lion-

charmed savannas five million years ago.
And began to tell ourselves
stories about things

we couldn't see. Gave up speed for height
and stood upright to scan the
horizon for dangers,

a trick impossible to unlearn even when
there are no dangers, even when
there are no horizons.

Everything we felt then is everything we
feel now. Which is why children
prefer to live in

tree houses and anxiety is the mother of
all religion. Why gardens
are so calming.

Our fathers who felt no fear did not
survive. They are not
our fathers.

II

A bonepit in Iraq 50,000 years old—high
pollen counts indicating flowers
had been thrown into

the grave on top of the body. The ones
who threw the flowers, they
are our fathers.

III

And the fall from grace? Mythicized memory
of our winsome life in the trees and
descent therefrom. Because

why would we leave such a paradise unless
cast out? Why leave the arboreal
delights—fruit and shade and

acrobatic sexual experiences—for the panicked
free-for-all of the open ground? Think
of it, our ancestors, the ones

who evolved our emotions for us, had to
worry about lions, plus whatever
lions worried about,

every moment of every day and night
for hundreds of thousands of
years. What would that

do to you? What has it done to us?
Made us mind-readers of every
emptiness. Imaginers

of the worst. Whereas up in the trees
we looked down on, we
laughed at the lions.

IV

It's thought the first villages formed only when
our ancestors refused to leave
their dead behind.

Graves, in other words, are what gave birth to
all our cities and all our cities
have given birth to.

## V

The very first artists painted on cave walls,
35,000 years ago. I wonder if
they were a sub-tribe of

flower-throwers. They chose to express them-
selves beneath the earth in caves.
What does that tell you?

Why would you descend to darkness to make
your art? Some archeologists think
they were shamans

who saw the cave wall as transparent mem-
brane between this and the
other world and

could call spirit-beings to the surface
in their paintings. I love most
the half-man half-beast—

elongated, floating, impossibly elegant
human form with a thin and
antlered head

and a raffish tail. He stares straight out
at the viewer. And who would
that have been?

## VI

I think all artists should first learn to paint
in caves before being allowed
to work above

ground. Then they'd know where their art
was coming from—and what
it was for.

## VII

50,000 years ago loneliness was a *real*
problem, because if you were
alone you'd probably

been left or cast out by the others and
you'd probably be eaten
and have no

flowers tossed over you nor ever be able
to give shape to your loneliness
on flickering

cave walls. A person at that time would
not wish to wander alone lost
in thought

over the grassy savannas or to meditate
upon the mysteries of life
exposed to the eyes

of predators. I wonder how many dreamy
proto-poets met their fate in
just such a way?

Another reason for underground art:
the heart grows bold in the
absence of lions.

## VIII

And yet dreaminess survives among us
and must therefore bestow
some evolutionary

advantage upon the dreamy. I'm reasonably
certain, however, I would
have been eaten.

## IX

Being savaged by lions must rank high
on the list of worst ways to die.
To look into

their eyes! In India even today, land where
the Buddha was born, hundreds
of people are killed

every year by tigers and lions. Children
mostly. One village lost seven
children in six

months. Special lion hunters are hired
to track and catch the man-
eaters but they

usually fail. The lions slither up at night
and steal the infants away to de-
vour them in the jungle.

I wonder what the insomnia situation
is like over there. Especially
for the mothers

and, of course, the children themselves.
I wonder how much Buddha
feared lions.

## X

I wonder if my own sleeplessness is tuned
to the long and lion-filled silences
our ancestors listened to.

My misery over the unreturned phone call
a testament to the still sharp fear
of being left forever.

## XI

Surface and depth! Everything is surface and
depth! Without plates shifting under
earth's surface

we would not be here. Which is a parable of
impalpable proportions. That under-
lying change changing

everything, ocean currents, planetary winds,
rainfall—shrinking African forests
and forcing us down

from the trees into the open. A casting out.
From which follows a smarter
pair of hands,

an ability to plan and remember and worry.
And to long for a paradise lost,
a lion-free world

where no one thought to cover themselves
with clothing because they were
already hidden.

A world where fruit had hardly to be reached for
it was so plentiful. A world we are
still falling from.

## XII

In South Africa, most hominid fossils are found
in limestone caves. And do you
know why? Were our

ancestors wise men, hermits who sank deeply
into the solitude of caves? Or were
they dragged there by lions?

## XIII

If you answered "dragged there by lions" you are
correct. The rise of cave-dwelling
hermit-monks

came much later. The great Tibetan poet Milarepa
lived in a cave for many years,
eating nettles and

meditating. Once a monster swirled its torments
upon him until inspired he put his
head into the demon's

mouth (a practice still observable today in many
circuses), and the demon disappeared.
But how did it feel

to sit in meditation at the site where hunger and
unmindfulness so intimately met?
Where real demons

dragged you to devour you? Well can I understand
how a religion devoted to paying
attention, to being

fully present, to wakefulness and impermanence,
would be born in such caves, among
nettles and bones.

## XIV

And how do the lions and tigers that ate our
ancestors show up in Buddhist
iconography?

As protectors, of course. But how do you turn
what you fear most into the keeper
of your safety?

## XV

Don't fly under false colors, for starters. Buddha
told his first followers to take their
robes from the newly

dead in the charnel grounds, but only the saffron
and brown worn by out-castes,
and advised them

that form was no other than emptiness, emptiness
no other than form. A truth they
slipped into fearfully,

I imagine. How would it change you to be thusly
attired? Probably lions wouldn't
even bother with you.

Stinking, empty-headed monks, triply cast out.
In Vermont, when eager, lost
Buddhist seekers came

through town asking where's The Tail of the Tiger?
The old-timers would tell them:
"About three inches

above its asshole." Better, I guess, than three inches
below. Though tiger shit, like everything,
is just illusion.

## XVI

To wrap yourself in the perceptions of others
and then enact the emptiness
of those perceptions.

Even a master illusionist is sometimes taken in
by reality—dragged offstage
in the tiger's mouth.

## XVII

"For the duck's legs, though short, cannot be
lengthened without causing dismay
to the duck." That's what

Chang-Tzu said, rendering all subsequent
philosophy an overcomplicated after-
thought. If you get that

one sentence, you need not read Kierkegaard
or Freud, not to mention Saint
Augustine or Kant.

Every tragedy in our history and in our own
ragged lives is triggered by
a willingness to

cause dismay to the duck. Or to the tiger,
who has a famously low tolerance
for being dismayed.

Chang-Tzu perceived the duckly nature
of the duck and did not wish it
were otherwise.

Whereas my own life is filled with birds
staggering around on stilt-like
legs. Unable to fly.

## XVIII

Because that's what you do when you stand
upright and free your hands
from locomotion—

you start grasping things and reshaping them,
turning the world into your
idea of the world.

# III

# Side by Side

# To Make the Wound More Beautiful

## George in New York

Inward, self-questioning, often unsure.
Often clearly miserable:
a kindred spirit, my nephew.
Readerly and melancholy.
The only other in my family
thus afflicted.
But the affliction is the way,
so I fed him books—
Salinger and Whitman,
the Greeks and ancient
Japanese poets,
Saigyō particularly.
Neruda of the odes,
of the wild undaunted
friendliness toward all things.
So that soon enough
he was taller than me,
handsomer, wiser,
gentler. When he came
to visit me in New York
I told him: "If I catch you
staring at the sidewalk
I'm sending you home."
After which he
noticed every bottle-
shard sculpture
in the East Village,
every brownstone gargoyle
in Park Slope,
and was seized by
the same depraved
exhaustion I always felt
anywhere near the corner
of Broadway and Canal.
Coming in from LaGuardia,
he'd tried to reason

the cabbie out of
a paranoid racist rant,
tried—between my shouts
and insults—calmly to
change his mind,
unwilling to give up
on anyone.
After I praised
his patience and intelligence,
he said he disliked
compliments, having inherited
the midwestern
clairvoyance for all signs
of arrogance
in himself or others.
I knew that feeling well,
but I told him, they're gifts,
it's ungracious not to
accept them.
And he seemed to accept that
and I complimented him
for doing so.
And then he shook off
his shyness like a fine black dust,
started talking to everyone—
jazz players after a set,
flea-market vendors,
fellow travelers on the subway.
Took his place in the world,
stepped into himself
and found he fit.
A wondrous thing to witness.
That will have been five
years ago this spring,
back when death was just an idea,
something to be spoken of
now and again.

* * *

My first thought when my brother called
was: This is going to happen and I
am going to die. When he called
from the hospital in Kyoto to tell me
his son George was worsening,
that his liver would fail,
that he needed a transplant
and I was the only viable donor—
my first thought was: This
is going to happen and I
am going to die.

And then I was on my way—
fearless and terrified,
watching a movie about
Dominican minor-leaguers
somewhere over the Pacific,
and life felt real, its strangeness
no longer half-hidden.

Six months before, I'd read a novel
about surgeons, its climactic scene
a harrowing, high-wire live
liver transplant between
twin brothers that saves
the recipient but kills the donor.
Why did I read that book,
why then? Past and future
inseparable, yes, I know.
But of all the books I might
have read, why that book, why then?

## First Meeting with the Surgeons

It was as if the helpless gods had convened
around a cluttered table to tinker
with fate one more time. I remember
how small the room seemed,
how unequal to tragedy or heroism,
the scuffed linoleum along the baseboards,
bookshelves overstuffed,
the unsteady chairs.
I remember Dr. Ogura,
the man who would cut me open
and delicately detach half my liver,
had a band-aid just above
his left eyebrow, and I wondered
had someone hit him, the parent
of a child who'd died in a failed
surgical procedure, a liver transplant
perhaps, or had he fallen
off his bicycle, or walked into
a doorjamb, or been gashed
by a low-hanging branch
while out for a Sunday stroll
in the hills above Kyoto?
You never see adults, or gods,
with band-aids on their faces,
but there he was, the injured surgeon.
And as he studied my blood tests
and explained the operation to me,
I couldn't stop thinking about it,
that cut above his eye, what
it looked like, how it happened,
what it might portend.

* * *

What is the sound of fear?

At Nijo Castle
the Shogun not only

surrounded him-
self with thick

walls and deep moats

he built the floors
to sing like night-

ingales underfoot
to warn him

of an enemy's approach.

* * *

When they walked me into the surgical theater,
I thought: This will be a little foretaste
of death, or possibly death itself.
I had told my brother, "If George lives
and I die, I can live with that."

And the night before, after we visited him,
jaundiced and unconscious in the ICU
but still handsome enough to make
the nurses fall in love with him,
and had touched his forehead and
said encouraging words to him, who knew
nothing of what was about to happen,
unless the body always knows
and the deep mind that listens even
when the shallow mind is fast asleep—
we passed Dr. Ogura in the hall
and he asked me, "Are you ready?"
"Yes," I said. "Are *you*?"

But when the moment comes,
all bravura vanishes, you just surrender.
The last thing I remembered
as they held the mask above my face
to put me under, to induce "a reversible lack
of awareness" (a fair description
of the human condition), was a sweet
young nurse smiling at me,
pumping her fists into the air,
as if in victory or exuberant bon voyage—
such a strange and beautifully incongruous image
before the world went dark.

* * *

Deep silence held him
and because he could not wake
I joined him there.

Nine hours our bodies lay
side by side, opened up,
while our absent spirits

did what? What did they do?
I like to think they
hovered together,

looked down on the carnage
below, the soft flesh
split apart, taken

and given, and that they forgave
each other for whatever
might happen,

held each other in the
dark and weightless ether
of the spirit world

before being called back
to the bloodied, bodied, spinning
world once more.

* * *

When his surgeon came to tell me, I was fussing
with a pillow, every move a whiplash of pain
and irritation. I felt my feet hanging
over the bed like two defeated fish, and thought:
This wasn't made for a six-foot-two Nebraskan.
And could the room have been designed so that
a person recovering from major abdominal surgery
might turn the lights on and off without
getting gingerly in and out of bed? Certainly not.
Miserable with my tiny unmanageable miseries
when Dr. Oiege came in, sat down and said:
"I have some very bad news. George suffered
a massive cerebral hemorrhage. I'm afraid
there's nothing we can do. He's brain dead."

* * *

They couldn't control his blood,
they said, though my liver started
working immediately

in his body. His brain
was swamped with blood,
though my liver started working.

Nothing could be done, they said.
After all we did, nothing could
be done. Because his brain

was swamped with blood.
Even with half a liver working
perfectly, nothing could be done,

and nothing can be done
now there is a bloody swamp
where consciousness had been.

* * *

Sleepless every night since the operation
I wandered the halls of the transplant ward,
pushing the coatrack-like contraption
that held my IV-drip, pain-med drip,
and three electrodes affixed to my chest
to track my untrustworthy heart.
My 3 a.m. walks became in time
a kind of walking meditation.
Nothing like major surgery
to keep you attentive to every step.
Of course my mind was still the darting
school of panicked minnows it had
always been. But once, as I came
to the end of the hall and looked out
the darkened window, I imagined
a sleepless monk somewhere
in the hills beyond the city
doing his own walking meditation,
making the same slow circles,
he around some pond or towering pagoda
and I around 30 or 40 wounded patients.
(In Japan an incision is a "wound.")
I imagined us mirroring each other,
like brothers, or like subatomic particles
split apart, apparently separate,
but spinning in perfect symmetry
no matter the space between.
I wondered if he was looking up
toward the hospital windows wondering
if someone there was thinking of him
and of the suffering we couldn't help but share.
And then I rounded the corner to begin
the long fluorescent journey
back to my room.

* * *

I wasn't there but my brother told me
that after they cut him loose
from all the machines,
let his body go like a small boat
drifting from the shore,
as my brother and his wife
held vigil beside the bed,
the doctors and nurses
who had served and tried
to save him came into the room
and stood in stillness for over
an hour until it was over—
until the strong young heart
stopped. He had been brain dead
for ten days but still with us,
rocking gently on the surface.
And then they all rode
the elevator down together,
the same elevator
we had taken up so many times,
big enough for gurneys and wheelchairs
and huge anxious silences.
And when his body had been
placed inside the hearse
that waited to enter the flurried stream
of Martumachi Street, they
bowed a long low bow, held it
until the car was gone.

* * *

I knelt beside his body the night before
we would consign it to the flames,
and read his journals, read his poems:

*May my foot find your doorstep,*
*that is why I walk each day.*

*May my hand move with yours,*
*that is why I write.*

*May I come home to your knowing,*
*that is why I live.*

How perfect and unlikely that death
should draw us together here in Kyoto,
where he'd come to teach and where
the poet we loved most, Saigyō,
lived and was cast out and wandered
these mountains in loneliness and rapture,
Saigyō, the warrior turned monk, who wrote:

*"Detached" observer*
*Of blossoms finds himself in time*
*Intimate with them—*
*So, when they separate from the branch,*
*It's he who falls . . . deeply into grief.*

* * *

So strange to think
a piece of me is already
buried in the air,
or exists as ashes
in an urn
mixed with his ashes,

and that when I'm ready
to make the final turn,
step through
the final wound
and leave this body,
part of me will be waiting there.

## From One Place to Another

We sat in the Yamatoya Jazz Bar,
such an unlikely place, dark
and soothing, deep in Kyoto,
its decor a cross between
a whorehouse and a 1970s
American basement—
red lampshades with gold
tassels, mismatched
sofas and chairs,
and thousands of LPs
shelved along red velvet walls.
My brother asked for Ellington,
"Take the A Train," by the shy,
continuously inspired
Billy Strayhorn.
Can you make a song
from instructions on
how to get from one place
to another? Yes.
Beer and ginger ale
is what we were drinking,
New York City what we
were thinking of—
my brother and I at The Fez
to hear the Mingus Big Band,
George and I at Barbés
to hear a Django guitarist.
Weeping is what we
were not doing, no elbows
on knees, faces in hands,
shoulders heaving—no,
we were taking a break
from all that, taking the A train
uptown to Harlem,
we stepped right up onto it
laughing as it lurched away
from the station nearly
knocking us
down.

* * *

Hobbled up
narrow cobble-
stone lanes
to the Pure
Land Buddhist
Temple
its haloed
half-smiling
Amitabha Buddha
perfectly placed
at the edge
of the graveyard
his hands
forming the
teaching mudra
as if to say
take heed
wake up
death comes
without warning.
Yes it does
I thought as I
looked out
over Kyoto
its thousand
ancient temples
and million
cramped apart-
ments—a city
like all cities
of the living
and dying
living together
side by side
one and the same.

* * *

Leaning over Sanjo Bridge
in mossy August light,
I imagine him
leaning here, looking
down on the lonely
Kamo River.
Maybe he saw the same
thin white crane
that stands and looks and
needles the shallow water.
Or another just like it.
Maybe he said to himself,
as I did: so they do
exist outside Zen paintings.
But where would he
have been going,
crossing this bridge from
one side to the other?
What thinking?
The smell of being
alone in a strange city—
would he have noticed that?
One more thing there
is now no way of knowing.

* * *

At Kiyomizu Temple
tourists clown
for the cameras

line up to catch
in a long-handled cup
its falling healing waters.

* * *

How I longed to be home—
such a roomy word:
"home." And here

I am

in this emptiness
with nothing to do but
rest and think and remember.

## Ultrasound

"Well," she said, "your incision is huge."
Yes, I wanted to say, I noticed that.
Or: You should see the other guy.
Though I did wonder how much bigger
than other scars my scar must have been
to shock a sixty-year-old radiologist.
Then she greased my crucified torso
and slid the camera over me
to photograph the lightning storms of pain
the 13-hour flight from Osaka
to Denver had unleashed again.
"The left lobe of your liver is gone," she said.
"There's nothing there." OK, I thought,
tell me something I *don't* know.
And then she did: "Did you have
a gallbladder before this surgery?"
"As far as I know," I said. "Well," she said,
"you don't have one now." "Jesus," I said,
my vast ignorance of the body surging up
into speech. "Can you live without that?"
"Oh, sure," she said, "you don't need it.
People have them taken out all the time."
But then I wondered what else
the good doctors in Kyoto failed to tell me,
or I failed to hear. Did I still have
an appendix, for example, or my tail-less
tailbone? Or any other ancillary
or vestigial organs the body
may have been born with?
And what about my totally superfluous
sense of impending doom? Or the not
strictly necessary or useful everlastingness
of all my wounds and regrets? Or my feeling
that failure might be a natural element
like water or air? Those were not removed,
were they? I don't think I could part
with them just yet.

## Update

Six months later
it's still the same:
I wake at 3 a.m.
my body hyper-
vigilant, as if
to say: Don't
cut me again.
And the sleep
meds—Restoril,
Valium, Lunesta,
Ambien? Candy
to my fearsome
sleeplessness.
They only make
me wish I had
the job of giving
drugs their names—
(a poet should
have that job)
like Adam
in the pharm-
aceutical garden

## Dr. Ogura

I'm glad I wasn't conscious
when they stapled me shut.
Do they use a staple gun?

No . . . and yet they must.
How else get them in?
I should have asked,

I guess, or possibly not.
But when Dr. Ogura took
them out, so skillfully

I could hardly feel it—
fifty-six of them clamped
along the incision

he'd opened—I asked him
why they used staples now
instead of stitches.

He paused, his hand poised
above my abdomen, then pulled
from his imperfect English

a perfect reply: "To make
the wound . . . more beautiful."

* * *

One moment keeps drifting back
above all the others,
unloosened from time's illusory flow:

how he stood in the Met
mesmerized before Van Goghs
and Monets and Pissaros

—as if held by some distant signal
from the source of beauty itself—

and asked in a breathless whisper,
"Are *those* the originals?"